BRITAIN
IN OLD PHOTOGRAPHS

DERRY
AROUND THE MAIDEN CITY

WESTERN EDUCATION AND LIBRARY BOARD LIBRARY SERVICE
& NORTH WEST ARCHAEOLOGICAL AND HISTORICAL SOCIETY

COMPILED BY
MAURA CRAIG, ROY HAMILTON, CHARLES LOGUE,
JANE NICHOLAS & RICHARD SINCLAIR

SUTTON PUBLISHING

Sutton Publishing Limited
Phoenix Mill · Thrupp · Stroud
Gloucestershire · GL5 2BU

First published 2003

Front endpaper: The courthouse, Bishop Street.
(*Mr Charles Logue*)
Back endpaper: Ferryquay Street. (*Bigger and
McDonald Collection*)

British Library Cataloguing in Publication Data
A catalogue record for this book is available from the
British Library.

ISBN 0-7509-3267-8

Typeset in 10.5/13.5 pt Photina.
Typesetting and origination by
Sutton Publishing Limited.
Printed and bound in England by
J.H. Haynes & Co. Ltd, Sparkford.

The Waterside seen from the city, 1920s. The view shows a fine group of commercial buildings in Foyle Street and Bridge Street. (*Mr Annesley Malley*)

CONTENTS

Butcher's Gate, the scene of fierce fighting during the Great Siege of Derry in 1689. It was rebuilt in 1866 and like both Bishop and Ferryquay Gates, this gate changed from being a simple defensive fortification to an ornamental monument dedicated to those who had fought in the siege to protect their city. (*Mr Charles Logue*)

INTRODUCTION

Derry, or Londonderry, is a majestic historic city located in the north-west corner of Northern Ireland. It is situated on the River Foyle and the mountains of Donegal provide an impressive scenic backdrop. Some of the city's characteristics are its steep streets, historic walls and its decorative and numerous handsome public buildings. Derry is considered one of the most historic, picturesque walled cities in Ireland and is the only one whose full circuit of ancient walls remains intact. The walls built between 1614 and 1619 have survived sieges in 1641, 1649 and the Great Siege of 1689. The fact that they have never been breached has resulted in the city commonly being referred to as 'The Maiden City'.

The name of the city popularly known as Derry or Londonderry is derived from the Irish 'Doire', which means a 'place of oaks' and it was among these oaks that Columcille founded his first abbey in AD 546. In honour of St Columcille, now regarded as the patron saint of Derry, the town was renamed 'Doire Colmcille' in the tenth century. This has become anglicised over the following centuries to Derry.

Derry was largely ignored by the English crown up until the mid-sixteenth century. But from then on there was increasing effort to bring Derry, and Ulster generally, under the rule of the anglicised central government. In 1609, under the direction of James I, a new plantation was devised, the aim of which was to ensure the creation of English and Scottish settlements in Ulster. In 1613 a development corporation of the city of London, the Honourable The Irish Society, was set up to ensure that Derry became the stronghold of English dominance in the north-west. It was at this stage that the name of the city changed, by charter, from Derry to Londonderry.

Between 1613 and 1619 the city walls were built under the guidance of the London-based the Honourable The Irish Society and the foundations of the modern city were laid. St Columb's Cathedral, a noted landmark in the city and a fine example of Ulster architecture, was constructed between 1628 and 1635, also under the management of the Honourable The Irish Society. It was the first post-Reformation cathedral built in Europe.

The most significant of the sieges against Derry took place in 1689. William of Orange, a Dutch man married to James II's Protestant daughter Mary, had been crowned King of England. His troops defended the city from King James II who was trying to make sure that Catholicism once again became the dominant religion throughout his kingdom. It was a group of Apprentice Boys who closed the gates as the army of King James II approached them and thus began the siege, which lasted 105 days. Eventually relief ships, bringing much-needed supplies, managed to sail up the river and break the series of booms laid across it. The blockade was over, but thousands were dead from disease and starvation. After this long and bloody siege the rebuilding of the dilapidated city took place and by 1800 a fine Georgian city had emerged 'the most picturesque of any place' (George Vaughan Sampson's *Survey of the County of Londonderry*, 1814).

The eighteenth century was a time of great economic growth and expansion in Londonderry. It was also during this period that the city became a port of economic significance. It built up extensive trading links with Britain, Europe and the colonies in America. The opening up of the British market to linen and agricultural produce allowed the city to use fully its strategic geographic position and become the natural place of export for produce from counties Donegal, Tyrone and Derry.

But it was people rather than produce that established Londonderry as the chief port for transatlantic trade. In this period emigration became an Ulster phenomenon. Between 1771 and 1772 6,300 emigrants sailed from the Derry port on 22 ships.

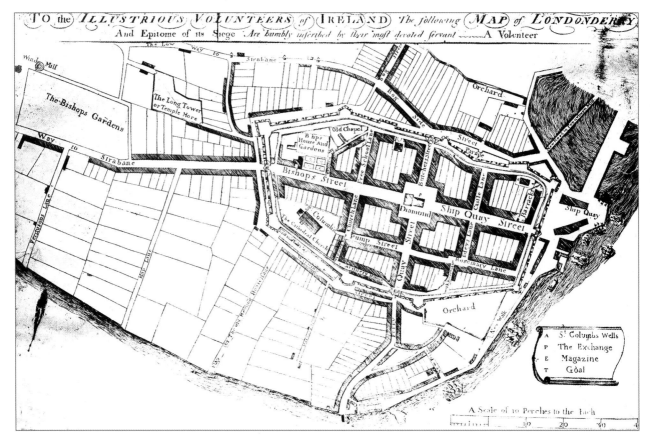

A map of Derry dating from the late eighteenth century that illustrates the cruciform layout of the city and shows the original four gates. It details the growth of the city as it spreads outwards from the 1-mile-circumference city walls. The River Foyle, flowing northwards to the sea, which became the main artery for trade, is visible, as is, to the west, the network of roads, which also contributed to the city's development. (*WELB*)

Increasingly the city was enjoying economic growth based on its success as a major port.

To a large degree the nineteenth century marked the industrial heyday of Londonderry. The city became a major producer of shirts. An industry grew up around this in the 1850s, and became the main employer in the city for the next 150 years. Of the people employed in the shirt factories, 90 per cent were women. Local man William Scott started the shirt trade in 1830. This was greatly expanded by a group of Scottish businessmen in the 1850s. These included William Tillie and John Henderson, whose red-brick factory Tillie & Henderson's, referred to in Karl Marx's *Das Kapital*, continues to dominate the entrance to the city from the Craigavon Bridge.

As a port, the ship-building industry also played a significant part in the city's economy. Between 1830 and 1924 four different yards were set up. One of the more successful yards was that operated between 1847 and 1870 by William Coppin. A creative, enterprising man, Coppin ran a thriving shipyard, which, at its height, employed over 500 people. The industry was revived again by Charles F. Bigger in 1886 and continued to be a major employer in the city right up to the 1920s.

Distilling whiskey was another industry with close links to Londonderry. Indeed, by 1900, the city not only had the largest distillery in Ireland but also was famous throughout the United Kingdom, the USA and Ireland for its whiskey.

At the beginning of the twentieth century Londonderry was a prosperous enterprising place. It was regarded as a city of opportunity, offering good employment prospects. With the opening of no less than four different railway lines in the nineteenth century, with a railway station at each corner of the Craigavon Bridge which spanned the River Foyle, it had an effective transport system and looked well placed to meet the challenges of the new century.

The city managed to sustain this economic growth until the years following the First World War. Derry's economic fortune then altered dramatically. In the changed world circumstances of the 1920s both the ship-building and distilling industries ceased in Derry. The shirt industry also faced increasing competition from cheap imports from Europe. Unemployment rose significantly. Emigration robbed the city of many of its inhabitants, lured by the chance of a better life elsewhere.

Although plagued by unemployment throughout the twentieth century and beyond, Londonderry continued to expand and enjoyed occasional highlights. The unscheduled landing of Amelia Earhart, the first woman to fly solo across the Atlantic in 1932, in the Shantallow area of the city caused much interest. This event has subsequently been commemorated in the city with the establishment of the Amelia Earhart centre. The arrival of the Canadian and especially the American servicemen during the Second World War provided a great deal of colour and excitement in the city. The steady influx of people and money from across the Atlantic helped the area to thrive during the war years. Airfields were constructed and the port was developed as a harbour, playing an increasing role in the war effort. In fact, the German U-boat fleet surrendered in Lisahally Harbour, at the mouth of Lough Foyle, at the end of the war.

In the late 1960s the political troubles, which were to blight the local landscape for the next three decades, erupted. The riotous confrontations that followed civil rights demonstrations eventually spilled over into open conflict with the emergence of 'No Go' areas in certain nationalist districts. Bloodshed, persistent rioting and disturbances were regular occurrences. In January 1972 Bloody Sunday, on which thirteen people died, occurred. To this day controversy rages regarding the events of this day and it is currently the subject of a public inquiry under Lord Saville.

With the ongoing violence in the streets of Londonderry, it was difficult to attract much-needed investment. However, and in spite of the troubles, the city continued to develop. New hotels, shopping centres, bars and leisure centres opened. The city, and many of its political representatives, were working hard to portray Londonderry as a vibrant and friendly place. But it was not only the politicians who were enhancing the city's reputation. Musicians of the calibre of Dana, Phil Coulter, Josef Locke and the Undertones, all natives of the city, undoubtedly helped to put The Maiden City on the map. The city was also justifiably proud of Nobel Prize winners John Hume and Seamus Heaney, who although not a native of the city was educated locally at St Columb's College.

The city has moved into the twenty-first century full of optimism. Although unemployment, sectarianism and social exclusion continue to bedevil Derry, there is real hope. The city is actively seeking and securing inward investment. The opening of the Millennium Complex, a cultural centre with a 1,000-seater auditorium and theatre, is regarded as the city taking its proper place as a major centre for culture and the arts. Bridging the religious divisions within the city will undoubtedly be a long and slow process. But perhaps the awareness of the divide and the need to move forward as a united community will hasten this process.

1
A Tour of the City

An aerial view of the city showing the Craigavon Bridge and two of the city's main factories, Tillie & Henderson's and Hamilton's shirt factories. (*Bigger and McDonald Collection*)

Ferryquay Gate, which was rebuilt in 1866 and is located at the top of Carlisle Road, an important arterial route from the Waterside into the city centre. It was this gate that the Apprentice Boys shut in the face of the Earl of Antrim's troops on 7 December 1688 to start the Great Siege of Derry. Close to Ferryquay Gate on the right-hand side was the Victoria Hotel, which was widely used by actors and actresses starring in the opera house in Carlisle Road. (*Mr Charles Logue*)

Bishop Gate, rebuilt as a triumphal arch by Henry Aaron Baker in 1789 on the centenary of the Great Siege and to the memory of King William III. During the siege the stretch of walls to either side of Bishop Gate was considered by the Jacobite forces to be the weakest link in the city's defences. Not surprisingly, most of the attacks were concentrated on this gate. (*Mr Charles Logue*)

Shipquay Gate, originally known as Water Gate and rebuilt between 1805 and 1808 in the same style as Butcher's Gate. A little to the north-west of it was the 'Coward's Bastion', which was removed to make way for a butter market. It is believed that it was over this part of the wall that Colonel Lundy escaped, during the Great Siege, dressed as a pauper. (*Mr Charles Logue*)

Bishop Street, which was originally known as Queen Street and was extensively destroyed in the Great Siege. On the left-hand side of Bishop Street is the headquarters of the Masonic Order. This building was the former Palace of the Protestant Bishops of Derry and Raphoe and was for some time the home of Mrs Cecil Francis Alexander, the famous hymn writer. (*Mr Charles Logue*)

St Columb's Cathedral, built between 1628 and 1633 by William Parrott and supervised by Sir John Vaughan, Governor of the City. It was constructed to meet the needs of the growing settler population for whom St Augustine's had become too small. The project was financed by the Honourable The Irish Society and cost £3,800 in total. In 1778 a spire was added and a slate roof fitted to replace the lead one. A process of restoration, renovation and repair has been ongoing ever since. (*Bigger and McDonald Collection*)

Of great architectural note in Bishop Street is the courthouse, which was erected in 1817 and modelled after the Temple of Erechtheus in Athens. It is adorned with Ionic pillars. (*Mr Charles Logue*)

Looking down Shipquay Street is the bronze statue of Sir Robert Alexander Ferguson, MP for the city, 1830–60, which was erected in the Diamond on 9 March 1863. Known locally as 'The Black Man', in 1927 this statue was moved to Brooke Park. Shipquay Street was formerly known as Silver Street and is renowned as one of the steepest streets in the British Isles. This road was home to two of the city's local newspapers, the *Londonderry Journal* and the *Standard*. It was in Shipquay Street that the acclaimed author Joyce Cary was born. (*Mr Charles Logue*)

This building in the Diamond was originally the town hall. It was built in 1692 and replaced in 1825 by a larger building. It remained the town hall until the opening of the Guildhall in Shipquay Place on reclaimed land in 1890. Between 1890 and 1908 it was used as an art school. (*Mr Charles Logue*)

The Diamond, from which four main streets, at right angles to each other, lead to the four original gates to the city – Shipquay, Ferryquay, Bishop's and Butcher's Gates. The Diamond was originally known as King William Square. For many years the town hall was located in the centre of the Diamond but this was demolished in 1910 and a garden was laid out on the site. In 1927 the war memorial, which was erected to commemorate the city's war dead, replaced this garden. (*Mr Charles Logue*)

Carlisle Road, *c.* 1910. This street was named after Lord Carlisle who also gave his name to the Carlisle Bridge, opened in 1863. The sheep walking on Carlisle Road would no longer be acceptable on this busy thoroughfare. There are two churches of particular note in this street – the Fourth Derry Presbyterian church, constructed between 1877 and 1879, and the Methodist church, which relocated to Carlisle Road in 1903. Also situated on Carlisle Road was the Welch Margetson & Co. shirt factory, which was considered to be one of the most impressive industrial buildings of Victorian Derry. (*Mr Charles Logue*)

Ferryquay Street, so-called because it led to the ferry by which people crossed the river. The street was originally called Gracious Street. At the corner of Ferryquay Street stands the large Edwardian building that has housed Austin's department store since it was built in 1906. Woolworths first opened its premises in Ferryquay Street after the First World War and remains there to the present day. (*Bigger and McDonald Collection*)

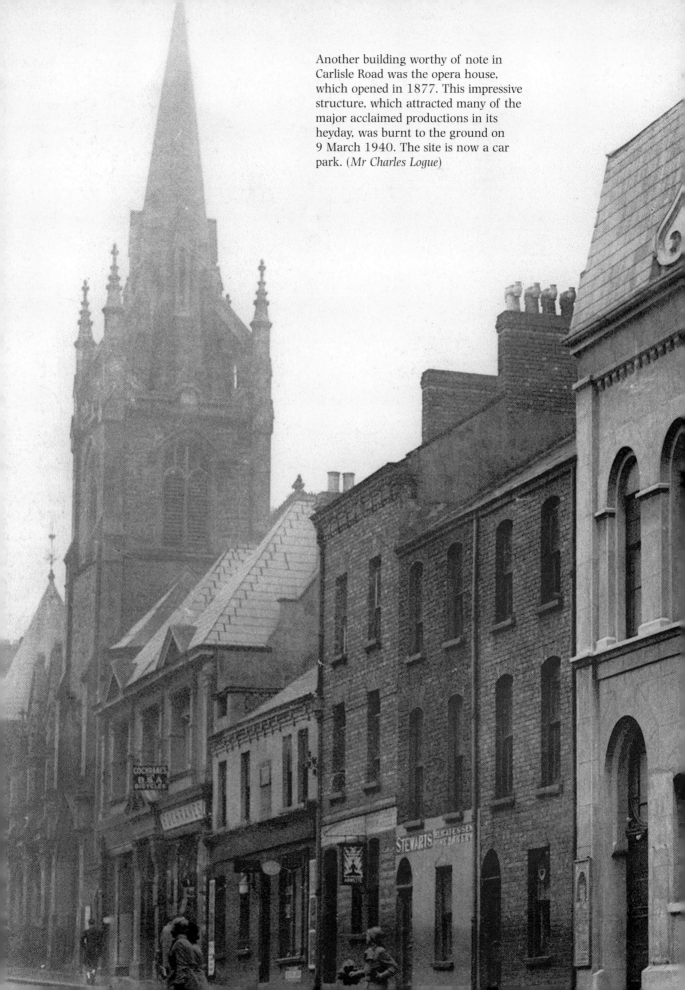

Another building worthy of note in Carlisle Road was the opera house, which opened in 1877. This impressive structure, which attracted many of the major acclaimed productions in its heyday, was burnt to the ground on 9 March 1940. The site is now a car park. (*Mr Charles Logue*)

Walker's Pillar, erected in 1826 in memory of the Revd George Walker, Governor of the City during the siege of 1689. The statue of George Walker was 9 ft high and in his right hand was a Bible, while the left extended towards the River Foyle. The column was blown up in 1973 and only its square Portland stone plinth remains. In the picture the monument is viewed from Nailor's Row, named because it was here that artisans made the nails for the wooden-hulled ships that were built on the River Foyle. (*Bigger and McDonald Collection*)

The jail, built in 1791 to the designs of Edward Miller. In 1798 Wolfe Tone was temporarily incarcerated in Derry jail after his capture in nearby Buncrana. Between 1819 and 1824 the prison was renovated and turrets were added to the frontage. The jail received notoriety on 20 March 1943 when twenty-one men made a daring early morning tunnel escape; twelve of these prisoners were later rearrested. The jail closed on 31 March 1953 and was demolished in 1971 to make way for a new housing development at the Fountain. (*Mr Don Morrison*)

Londonderry is the last city in Ireland to be encircled by walls; in fact, it is the only city or town in Ireland where the original walls remain intact. Two buildings of note in Shipquay Place are the Northern Bank, right, and next to it the Northern Counties Hotel. The bank was built to the designs of Thomas Turner in 1866 and is considered one of his best commercial designs. The Northern Counties Hotel was built in 1902, and it was here that Amelia Earhart dined after her solo flight across the Atlantic. (*Mr Charles Logue*)

The Guildhall, the foundation stone of which was laid in 1887. It was opened in 1890 at a cost of £20,000. After the fire in 1908 the Guildhall was rebuilt to the designs of M.A. Robinson. It was extensively refurbished after bomb damage in 1972. The clock tower is one of the biggest of its kind in Ireland. (*Mr Charles Logue*)

The Guildhall was burnt on Easter Sunday, 1908. The fire was described by the local newspaper the *Derry Journal*, as the 'greatest fire ever witnessed in Derry within living memory'. (*Ulster Folk and Transport Museum*)

St Eugene's Cathedral. The Revd Dr Kelly laid the foundation stone of St Eugene's Cathedral on 26 July 1851. The cathedral was dedicated on 4 May 1873 and cost upwards of £50,000. It was another thirty years before the magnificent 256-ft-tall spire was added. The cathedral was solemnly consecrated on 21 April 1936, by which time all debt had been cleared. (*Mr Charles Logue*)

The Municipal College, Strand Road. E.J. Toye designed the building, known locally as the Tech, in 1908. An impressive four-storey structure, it has been greatly extended over the decades. It is now called the North West Institute of Further and Higher Education and has a number of outreach centres throughout the city. (*Mr Pearse Henderson*)

Magee College, originally set up in 1865 as a Presbyterian Theological and Liberal Arts College. It is named after Mrs Martha Magee, the wife of a Dublin Presbyterian minister, whose bequest of £20,000 helped establish the college. The main Gothic-style buildings date from that period. There was great controversy in the 1970s when the government of Northern Ireland decided to situate the new University for Ulster in Coleraine rather than at Magee. By the 1980s, however, Magee College began to develop and the number of students has now swelled to over 3,000. (*Mr Pearse Henderson*)

Foyle College, Lawrence Hill. This school was built in 1814 having relocated from its original site in Society Street. It was constructed there in 1617 and was then known as Derry Free Grammar School. A protestant boys' grammar, the college amalgamated with the former Girls' Londonderry High School in the 1970s to become a co-educational institution known as Foyle and Londonderry College. This school has had many distinguished pupils including the songwriter Percy French, the revolutionary John Mitchell and the Restoration dramatist George Farquhar. (*Mr Pearse Henderson*)

St Columb's College, Bishop Street. On Monday 3 November 1879 'Saint Columkille's College' opened to day pupils and boarders. The college was built in the grounds of the residence of Bishop Hervey, the 4th Earl of Bristol and the Bishop of Derry from 1768 to 1803. The school incorporated the Casino (Italian for 'summerhouse'), which was built for Hervey, and also the remains of a seventeenth-century windmill, which played a part in the Great Siege of Derry. The school has since moved to a new location. St Columb's will undoubtedly be remembered for its two Nobel Prize winners – John Hume and Seamus Heaney. (*Mr Pearse Henderson*)

The River Foyle and the quay, which played an important part in the city's ship-building industry and as a major trading and emigration port. It is estimated that 200,000 emigrants passed through the city's port in the first seventy years of the nineteenth century. The Waterside, situated on the east bank of the city, has grown significantly over the last twenty years. The troubles have resulted in a considerable movement of Protestants from the Cityside with the majority of the Protestant population of the city now located in the Waterside. (*Mr Charles Logue*)

Carlisle Bridge. At the beginning of the nineteenth century it was decided that Derry needed a new bridge to accommodate the growing requirements of a developing community. George William Frederick, Earl of Carlisle, opened this bridge for traffic on 24 September 1863. It was named after him and was 1,180 ft long and 30 ft wide, with two decks. When it opened the Carlisle Bridge was regarded as the most beautiful structure of its kind in the United Kingdom. (*Mr Charles Logue*)

The Craigavon Bridge, opened in July 1933. This bridge was built alongside the Carlisle Bridge and was similar in appearance. Between March and July 1933 both bridges operated side by side, but as soon as the two decks of the Craigavon Bridge were completed plans were made for the demolition of the Carlisle Bridge. Built by Dorman, Long & Co., Craigavon Bridge cost £255,510. (*Mr Charles Logue*)

Ebrington Barracks. The original barracks were situated in Foyle Street but by 1839 were replaced by Ebrington Barracks, named after Viscount Ebrington, Lord Lieutenant of Ireland. During the First World War soldiers from the 1st Battalion of the Cheshire Regiment left Ebrington to fight and die in Belgium at the Battle of Mons. During the Second World War the base, known as HMS *Sea Eagle*, played an important part in the Battle of the Atlantic and a joint Royal Navy/Royal Air Force Anti-Submarine Training School was established there in 1940 and remained until 1970. (*Mr Ian Bartlett*)

Duke Street, a thriving retail area until the mid-1960s. At this time the construction of a new road system saw the demise of the street as the main trading area in the Waterside. In its heyday this street contained one of the city's main bakeries, Eaton's, as well as Meehan's distillery and the famous saddlers Rodgers'. (*WELB*)

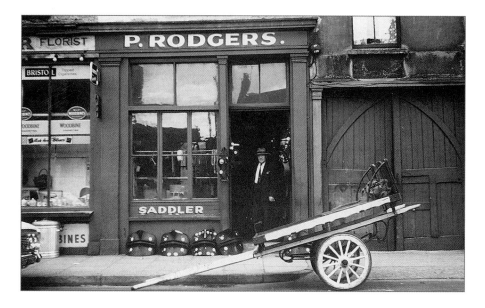

Peter Rodgers, the saddler, in the doorway of his shop in Duke Street. (*Miss Mabel Colhoun*)

St Patrick's Hall, known affectionately as The Pat's Hall. It was opened originally as a parochial hall for the local Catholic church and was a popular meeting place for the young people of the Waterside, who enjoyed many ceilithe there. St Patrick's Hall was also the headquarters of the boys' club. It was demolished in the 1980s. (*Mr Charles Logue*)

Victoria Hall, built in 1913 on the site of a temperance hall, which dated from the mid-nineteenth century. The Orange Order used it until it became the Services Club in the late twentieth century. (*Mr Charles Logue*)

The Workhouse, Glendermott Road, was opened on 10 November 1840 with accommodation for 800 inmates. Its aim, along with many similar institutions across the country, was to house the destitute. (*WELB*)

The interior of the workhouse. In order to discourage lengthy stays, conditions inside the workhouse were stark and the regime was harsh. On entering the establishment inmates were stripped of their clothes, given a prison-like uniform and segregated according to sex and age. The workhouse closed in 1947 and the building was then used as a hospital. A workhouse museum and public library has now been opened on the site. (*WELB*)

Altnagelvin Hospital. It
was built in 1960 and was
the first major acute
hospital to be completed in
Europe after the Second
World War – at a cost of
£2,680,000. (*Bigger and
McDonald Collection*)

Statues in Waterloo Place.
Derry has always been
associated with emigration
and these bronzes were
erected to commemorate the
many emigrants who passed
through the port of Derry.
(*Mr Ian Bartlett*)

2
Social History

Two children at Limavady railway junction about to board the train to Londonderry en route to the tender, which would take them to the liner off Moville, *c.* 1930s. The young girl is carrying the 'Stars and Stripes' flag and this would seem to indicate that their intended destination was the USA. Londonderry was the port of departure for emigrants from all over the north-west of Ireland. (*Bigger and McDonald Collection*)

A family about to start their journey from Derry to the New World, *c.* 1900. Many of the emigrants departing from the quay in Derry came from Donegal and Tyrone as well as Derry itself, driven to emigration by poverty and lack of employment prospects at home. (*Bigger and McDonald Collection*)

FOR
QUEBEC.

THE WELL KNOWN SHIP
LONDONDERRY
CAPTAIN TOWERSON,
To Sail about the 5th of April.

This Ship is on her Passage from St. JOHN, N. B., to this Port, and expected to arrive next week. She will be fitted up in the best manner for Passengers, and the usual allowance of Bread or Bread Stuffs, given without charge.

For Passage apply to the Owners,
J. & J. COOKE.
Londonderry, March 17, 1846.

☞ The Cargo of this Ship, consisting of Birch Timber, and Deals, from 8 to 24 feet in length, 7, 9, and 11 Ins. in breadth, for sale on Moderate Terms, on arrival.

An advertisement promoting emigration to Quebec, 1846. (*Londonderry Journal*)

The *Cameronia*. At the bottom of Bridge Street was the jetty where the tenders of the Anchor Line took emigrants to Moville to board the liners that left weekly for the USA. The *Cameronia* was one such liner, which regularly ferried emigrants from Derry to the USA. (*Mrs Carlin*)

Bridge Street, *c.* 1910. For many emigrants the boarding houses in Bridge Street, located close to the quay, were where they spent their last night on Irish soil. The triangular sign attached to the wall indicates that there was a handball court at the rear of the premises. One of these establishments has been rebuilt as an exhibit in the Ulster American Folk Park near Omagh. This street has now been partially demolished and the Foyleside shopping centre has been built in its place. (*Bigger and McDonald Collection*)

Shipquay Place, *c.* 1900. Public transport in the city was by jaunting car or tram – McMonagle's Long Car in the centre foreground brought passengers from the Lough Swilly railway terminus up the Strand Road to the city centre. The Northern Counties Hotel (second building from the right) is under construction. The aerials are coming from the telegraphy department of the post office behind the Northern Counties Hotel and were used to send and receive telegrams. The Golden Teapot hanging outside McCullagh's grocery store was a famous local landmark for many years. (*Mr Charles Logue*)

Foyle Street decked out for the visit of King Edward VII and Queen Alexandra, 28 July 1903. In this photograph the tea merchant's premises of R.J. Black, who founded the City of Derry Presbyterian Working Men's Institute in the Diamond, is seen. (*Derry City Council, Heritage and Museum Service*)

The School of Art decorated for the king and queen's visit, July 1903. The statue in front of the building is that of Sir Robert A. Ferguson, MP for Londonderry between 1830 and 1860. It now stands at the entrance to Brooke Park. The hall was demolished in 1910 and a garden of remembrance was laid out on the site. (*Derry City Council, Heritage and Museum Service*)

The Rabble, 1930s. The Rabble was the name given to hiring fairs in Tyrone, Donegal and Derry. In nearby Limavady it was called the Gallop. Local farmers came to recruit agricultural workers and domestic servants for the subsequent half year. Wages were poor and those who sold their labour were often very young. It was a big day for Derry traders with large crowds assembling in the Diamond area of the city from early morning. Hiring fairs were held six times a year on the three successive Wednesdays after 12 May and 12 November. (*Mr Tony Crowe*)

Waterloo Street, 1950s. Dan Doherty, known as Scotch Dan, owned this second-hand clothes shop, one of many in Waterloo Street. The youngest child in the photograph, in the pram, is Dan Doherty's grandson, Danny McCloskey. The two boys are the Plummer brothers. Walker's Pillar is in the background. (*Mr Charles Logue*)

Amelia Earhart in Derry with members of the McLaughlin family and Dan McCallion, 1932. Amelia Earhart flew her red Lockheed Vega 2,000 miles across the Atlantic in just under 15 hours which made the 34-year-old pilot world famous and some £60,000 richer. She landed about 4 miles from the city in a field in Ballyarnett. A local department store owner, Larry Hasson, was there that day and still talks about the excitement of the occasion. Just five years later in 1937 Amelia disappeared without trace while flying over the Pacific Ocean. (*University of Ulster Library*)

General Balbo, the Italian Air Minister in Mussolini's Fascist government, is seen here with Mayor Dudley McCorkell during a short visit to Derry in July 1933. The flying boats of the Italian Air Armada refuelled in Derry en route to the Centennial Exhibition in Chicago. Refuelling facilities had been set up at Lisahally for them. General Balbo was leading an investigation into weather conditions in the area and his visit was welcomed by the small Italian community in Derry. It was the cause of much excitement in the city. (*Bigger and McDonald Collection*)

Eamon De Valera, leader of Fianna Fail in the Republic of Ireland, on a visit to Derry in 1951. He came, without a civic invitation, to open a festival of Gaelic culture and sporting events. However, he was very warmly welcomed with people surging towards his car and almost swamping him. For many it was an honour to have one of the leaders of the 1916 Easter Rising in their midst. (*Mr Bobby Upton*)

The Eucharistic Congress, 1932. This event was a major Roman Catholic celebration held at various venues around the world since 1881. It was intended to deepen understanding and devotion to the Eucharist and in 1932 came to the Phoenix Park, Dublin. This occasion was celebrated locally – each street had its own arch and any household that owned a wireless allowed others to hear the mass at which Count John McCormack sang. This photograph is of Nelson Street in the old Bogside, now redeveloped. (*Mr Michael Gillespie*)

An Orange arch in Cuthbert Street, *c.* 1920. As part of the 12 July celebrations it was often common for the residents of various streets to construct decorative arches. The 12 July is the date on which the Orange Order traditionally celebrate the victory of William III over King James II at the Battle of the Boyne in County Louth. (*Mr Charles Logue*)

The funeral of William McGahey passing the jail on its way to the City Cemetery, 1933. Billy McGahey was a sergeant major in the 10th Inniskillings in the First World War. He was stationed in Dublin during the 1916 Rising and as a Unionist Justice of the Peace in Derry was noted for his fairness and justness to all. His home, now demolished, was in Fountain Street and his descendants still live in the city. (*Bigger and McDonald Collection*)

Cremation of Keher Singh, New Year's Day, 1940. Prior to the building of a crematorium in Belfast cremations would normally have been carried out in Glasgow. The onset of war, however, meant that travel for this purpose was no longer permitted. Arrangements were made to hold the ceremony in Eglinton, a few miles outside the city. Among those seen here are Mr Mohabat Vij (ninth from left), Mr Chada (eighth from left), Mr Sumra (sixth from left) and Mr Singh (third from right). (*Ms Charlotte Vij*)

Hobnails in Brooke Park, 1930s. The children are, from left, Tommy Fox, Thomas McCourt and P.J. Kelly. Gwyns Institute in Brooke Park has served many community needs. Originally an orphanage, it has housed a museum, a welfare clinic, the main library for the city, a workshop for the blind and during the war years it was the assembly point for the civil defence. Within Brooke Park itself there are many recreational facilities such as tennis courts, football pitches and children's playgrounds. It is of little surprise then that Brooke Park is widely regarded as the 'People's Park'. (*Bigger and McDonald Collection*)

The Girl Guides on their way to a Young People's Rally in First Derry Presbyterian church, *c.* 1930s. (*Mr Tony Crowe*)

Long Tower Carnival, 1952. The carnival was organised to raise money for the Derry Catholic Building Fund (DCBF). The parade is seen here in Rossville Street, passing the bar owned by the Boyce family. The money raised was for the construction of Catholic schools and churches and was a vital source of funding. (*Mr Charles Logue*)

The last Londonderry and Lough Swilly train, 1954. The train is seen coming into Derry from Buncrana at the level crossing in Strand Road. The Londonderry Shipyard premises, now Fort George, are in the background. The trees line the Culmore Road where George Maxwell, who owned the Northern Counties Hotel, lived in Troy Hall. Sir Robert Ferguson, former MP for the city, also had a home in this street. (*Mr Don Morrison*)

Springtown Camp, 1942. This camp was built for the American servicemen who were reported to be in the city, incognito, one year prior to the bombing of Pearl Harbor in December 1941, when the USA officially entered the war. Many were from the Construction Battalion and did not wear uniforms or identify themselves as American servicemen until after December 1941. They were responsible for the building of a secret underground bunker in Magee University. It was widely believed that if Derby House, Liverpool, the communication base for the Atlantic, had been bombed, Magee would have taken over its role. (*Mr Leo Coyle*)

Springtown Camp, 1950s. At the end of the Second World War the American servicemen left and the huts at the camp were quickly filled up with families from every part of Derry. Springtown Camp became home to over 300 families and remained in existence until 1967, when the last 2 families were housed. (*Mrs Stanley*)

A garden party at Boom Hall, 1898. Mayor J.B. Johnston and his wife are the hosts of this event to honour the Honourable The Irish Society, which visited the city every year. David Cleghorn Hogg, seventh from the left in the front row, had just opened a new shirt factory on Great James Street. In 1913 he was to become Liberal MP for the city. (*Derry City Council, Heritage and Museum Service*)

A sad photograph of one of Derry's best-known country houses, Boom Hall, in 1990. The building remains derelict today. It stands about 2 miles from the city where the boom was thrown across the Foyle during the Great Siege of 1689. It was built in 1770 and later became the home of members of the Cooke family, a famous family partnership in the shipping trade. (*WELB*)

A hunt at the White Horse Inn, Campsie, a few miles from the city, *c.* 1938. The White Horse accommodated coaches, horses and travellers. (*Bigger and McDonald Collection*)

City and County Hospital, 1924. Built in the early nineteenth century, the hospital, which served both city and county, was known locally as the Infirmary and had an excellent reputation. In this photograph the building is decorated for the visit of the Duke and Duchess of York, later King George V and Queen Elizabeth (subsequently the Queen Mother). In the early twentieth century a serum to combat diphtheria had become available in the hospital, thus giving doctors great encouragement and drastically reducing childhood mortality. (*WELB*)

LOCAL BLIND
PROTEST
MARCH

OUR FIGHT IS AGAINST BAD CONDITIONS
UNSANITARY WORKSHOP & INADEQUATE PAYMENT
OUR CAUSE IS FOR DECENT SUPPORT
WILL YOU SUPPORT OUR CAUSE

BLIND —
BUT NOT TO THE HARD FACTS OF LIFE

The blind protest march, 1950s. Seen here coming down Creggan Street from Brooke Park, these protesters are a harsh reminder that the 1950s were hard times for disabled workers. (*Mr Tony Crowe*)

Scotch boat, 1960s. To the older generation of the city the heart left the port of Derry when the Scotch Boat made its last sailing in the autumn of 1966. The service lasted 140 years and was linked initially with the rise of the shirt industry. Derry to Glasgow was the first industrial export market in the north-west. Increasingly, the Scotch boats were used to export animals – cattle and pigs were shipped weekly. For the many people obliged to go to Scotland to find work, it was a possible, if a little uncomfortable, means of travel. (*Mr Annesley Malley*)

Geese going to slaughter on their way to Scotland, 1930s. Geese were walked the 18 miles from Park village to the city quay to be shipped to markets in Glasgow. Before starting the journey, their feet were put through tar and then sand to protect them. Seen here outside the Harbour Museum, these healthy specimens would have provided Christmas dinner for Scottish households. (*University of Ulster Library*)

Charles Nash, who enjoyed a glittering career in both amateur and professional boxing. Born in the
Creggan Estate, Nash reached the pinnacle of his amateur career in 1972 when he, along with another
local boxer Neil McLaughlin, took part in the Munich Olympics. (*WELB*)

Oak Leaf Athletic Club at the Lisburn Cup, 1965. This local athletics club enjoyed considerable success in track and field and cross-country events. Back row, left to right: Hubert Logue, Christy McMonagle, Paddy McLaughlin, Jimmy Logue, Charlie Bell, Felix Cunningham, Tommy Mullan, James Heaney; front row: Willie Deery, Charlie Fox, Gerry Craig, Jim Doherty, Redmond Brown. (*Mr Gerry Craig*)

Presentation to Paul Craig, winner of the Derry marathon in 1983. He had won the Belfast marathon four weeks earlier and in the Derry event he achieved the fastest time ever previously recorded for a marathon in Northern Ireland. Also seen here are his mother Mrs Maisie Craig, his nephew Sean Paul Dillon and Mayor David Davis (the gentleman with the moustache). (*Mr Gerry Craig*)

Runners in the women's mini marathon, June 1984. This was to be the first of many 'Female Fives' organised to raise funds for the Foyle Hospice by Dr Tom McGinley. Over 2,000 female competitors ran from the Waterside to the city centre in a carnival atmosphere. It was one of the biggest mass-participation events ever organised in the city. Seen here are Carmel Mullan (964) and her sister Mary Kay Mullan (965) passing Dacre Terrace and the Abercorn Factory. (*Mr Eamon Melaugh*)

International Triathlon, June 1995. The city welcomed the world's leading triathletes who had come to Derry to participate in the World Cup Triathlon which was staged around the city centre. A significant day in the city's sporting history, this event attracted a crowd of 25,000 and was beamed to 250 million television viewers around the world. The event was won by two Australian triathletes, Brad Beven in the male category and Emma Carney in the female category. (*Mr Gerry Lynch*)

Overleaf: City of Derry Football Club, 1931/32. When this season opened the team took the field in a new strip – a white shirt replaced the claret and sky blue that had been worn previously. In 1934 the red and white strip was introduced, identical to Sheffield United, possibly in honour of Billy Gillespie, Derry City's player-manager who had captained United to English Cup triumph in 1929. E.D.R. Shearer (inset) was a great all-round sportsman, also being an international cricketer. (*Mr Charles Logue*)

DERRY

Top Row : S. FOSTER   W. GILLESPIE   MASON   HARKIN
(Assistant Secretary)   (Player-Manager)

Lower Row :   COMMON   FERGUSON   FORSTER

(Inset)   E. D. R. SHEARER

Y F.C.

Published by MADDEN BROS. DERRY
(Copyright)

TON   DUBOIS   BARRIE   C. GLENN
(Trainer)

NELIS   KELLY   McCANN   R. MARTIN

The Thiepval Memorial Band marching with Derry City Football Club, April 1964. In 1964 Derry City won the Irish League Championship for the first time. This event was celebrated in great style with all bands in the city invited to take part in a victory parade. The band is seen here at the bottom of Abercorn Road, having left the Brandywell Showgrounds to parade over Craigavon Bridge, up Spencer Road and Simpson's Brae then back to the Diamond. (*Mr Joe Nicholas*)

A City of Derry Rugby Club team, 1960s. The City of Derry Rugby Club was established in 1881 and has enjoyed considerable success over the last 120 years. It has recently moved to new premises at Judges Road on the outskirts of the city. It is a sport that continues to grow in popularity in the city. Back row, left to right: John Logan, Norman Duddy, Ken Gamble, Ivan McNally, Robert Dunn, George Tees, Robin Smith; front row: Alastair Kincade, Wilson McGonigle, Ian Jackson, John Arthur, Ken Bond, George Hayes, Jack Wilson. (*Mr Ken Gamble*)

The City of Derry Cricket Club, 1937. The club was formed in 1907 and enjoyed considerable success in the 1920s and 1930s. In 1939 the club went into decline with many of its key members participating in the war effort. However, the club, despite its ups and downs, in its ninety-five-year history has built up a great tradition in the game and has contributed much to north-west of Ireland cricket. Back row, left to right: S. Combe, H. Bond, G. Gallen, G. Stewart, N. McConaghey, F. Moore, J. Gallen (Umpire); front row: H. Chambers, W. Robinson, F. Chambers, G. Black, –?–. (*Mr W.H.W. Platt*)

A tennis party in Brooke Park, 1920s. This type of gathering was a popular pastime and there were many clubs around the city. (*University of Ulster Library*)

Derry Rowing Club with the Regatta Cup, 1930s. Included in this photograph are Mr Eric Phillips, Mr Thomas Stringer and Mr Harold McCullagh, of Golden Teapot fame. The club's headquarters were on the quay – the aptly named Boating Club Lane. A regatta was held annually, where local and visiting teams competed on the Foyle. (*Mr Charles Logue*)

3
Work

Workers at Hogg & Mitchell's shirt factory celebrating Queen Elizabeth's visit to the city in 1953. For a century and a half shirt making was the most important industry in Derry. In the 1920s Derry had over 40 factories which employed some 8,000 people. By 1980 this number had quartered. (*Mrs Thelma McDonnell*)

The employees of the Star shirt factory, *c.* 1950. (*Mr T. McQuilkin*)

In June 1919 the Liverpool photographers Sir Joseph Causton & Sons were commissioned to record the shirt-making operations within the City Factory. This was the cutting room. The cloth was brought here and the material was hooked up into the right lengths and the various parts of the shirt were marked using cardboard patterns. The cloth was then cut, often by the male employees. The neckbands, fronts and cuffs were usually cut with a hand-knife, while the bodies and sleeves were done with a small power-knife. (*University of Ulster Library*)

The sewing department, 1919. The working environment inside the factory was very noisy and conversations had to be carried out above the clatter of the sewing machines. Every shirt was handled by a total of eight workers with each individual specialising in a particular aspect of production. (*University of Ulster Library*)

The ironing department, 1919. Many of the shirt factories did their own laundering. After soaping, rinsing and blueing the shirts were starched and sent to the drying room. Finally they reached the ironing room. The irons used were heated by gas. Derry had the reputation of possessing a highly trained body of expert ironers. The Derry shirt was famous for its 'whiteness', a quality attributed to the local water used in the laundering. (*University of Ulster Library*)

Starch dollies, cylindrical tubs in which the shirts were starched, in use at a shirt factory, 1930s. (*Bigger and McDonald Collection*)

Workers coming out of Tillie & Henderson's shirt factory, once one of the biggest shirt factories in the world, 1960s. Famed for its mention in Marx's *Das Kapital* as an example of one of the worst effects of the factory system, Tillie & Henderson's was a major employer in the city right up to its closure in 1972. Despite Marx's comments, conditions in this factory were relatively good and it was generally regarded as a great place to work. (*University of Ulster Library*)

Tillie & Henderson's, 1999. Built in 1856 the company's large red-brick factory was one of the early works of the architect John Guy Ferguson. Conservation groups were working to preserve it before it was extensively damaged by fire in December 2002 and had to be demolished. (*Mr Roy McCullagh*)

Watt's Distillery at Abbey Street, 1918. Mr David Watt acquired the distillery in 1839 and the business became a major employer of men in the city. There was also a distillery in Duke Street in the Waterside, taken over by Watt's in 1870. A distillery situated in Pennyburn closed in 1840. The one at Abbey Street was among the best-known in the United Kingdom. In 1902 the Abbey Street and Duke Street concerns amalgamated and became known as United Distillers. By 1921, however, as the price of whiskey soared, the Abbey Street distillery had closed. (*Mr Charles Logue*)

Duke Street, 1950. Once a vibrant busy street, Harper's Boots and Shoes Manufacturers was one of the many industries located here. They were the only manufacturers of boots and shoes in the north-west and enjoyed a deserved reputation far beyond the Derry area. 'Shamrock' was the brand name on all their products. (*Bigger and McDonald Collection*)

Delivering milk, 1930s. This man is an employee of one of the Donegal milk vendors who travelled around Derry selling milk. (*Mr Tony Crowe*)

One of Brewster's horse-drawn delivery vans outside the factory, 1904. The production of biscuits became commercially viable from about 1880 with the invention of the machines needed to make them. By 1930 four of the six biscuit factories in Ireland were in Northern Ireland and Brewster's Ltd, Londonderry, was one of the leading manufacturers. J.P. Brewster, who founded the factory, was a former City High Sheriff and his company's extensive premises were in Little James Street. Brewsters also baked bread and in the early days of the twentieth century this was distributed by a horse-drawn van. (*University of Ulster Library*)

Workers rolling bacon in one of the pork stores in Derry, c. 1912. The largest employers of male labour after the closure of the North of Ireland Shipbuilding Company Limited in 1924 were the local pork stores. The bacon curing industry is one of the oldest in the city and extant records show that the first products were shipped to England in 1774. Bacon rolling was a practice begun in the pork houses in the city in the 1840s. (*Bigger and McDonald Collection*)

Farm workers harvesting oats, 1939. A labour-intensive activity, and very weather-dependent, oats were tied into sheaves then four of these were made into a stook, tied together at the top. This was a companionable activity as groups of binders followed the reaper across the field. In this photograph the workers are men, but both reaping and binding were often done by women. (*Londonderry Sentinel*)

Teatime in the harvest field of Mr J. Watson, Bolies, Londonderry, 1940s. (*Mr Tony Crowe*)

The Craigavon Bridge under construction, 2 October 1931. Cranes are working on the ironwork of the old Carlisle Bridge, which was to be replaced by the Craigavon Bridge. (*Mott MacDonald Photo Library*)

The Craigavon Bridge under construction, 4 January 1932. Considerable progress has been made since the photograph above was taken. The bridge was officially opened in July 1933. (*Mott MacDonald Photo Library*)

A diver in the Foyle helping with the construction of the Craigavon Bridge, *c.* 1931. This was a dangerous undertaking, as foundations had to be sunk deep into the river bed, a job that had cost the lives of four men working on the construction of the Carlisle Bridge in 1861. This professional diver came from Scotland and is seen here with the men who assisted him. Included in the photograph is Mr Ned Farren from neighbouring Ballykelly. (*Reproduced with permission of the National Museums and Galleries of Northern Ireland*)

Middle Quay, 1890. It was from here that the Garrison ferry conveyed passengers to the Waterside. (*Mr Charles Logue*)

Derry Quay, 1950s. Derry has been a major trading port for well over 200 years. Throughout this period dockers have been the lifeblood of the port and a highly respected body of working men. In 1963 over 500 dockers were employed and the tradition of dockers, in certain families, ran through many generations. But in the last decade with the move of the port to Lisahally, on the outskirts of the city, and modern technology used in the loading and unloading of cargoes, few Derry men continue to earn their living as dockers. (*Mr Charles Logue*)

Checking the grain at the weights office on the quay, 1920s. The man on the far right is Thomas McGlinchey. (*Mrs Tricia Ward*)

Workers upgrading the wharfs on Derry's quay, *c.* 1940. Similar timbers have been used for the construction of the new public artwork by Locky Morris erected to commemorate the many emigrants who left from the city. This is situated in the grounds of the Derry City Council Offices. (*Mr Leo Coyle*)

The Hill & Co. shop, 1908. Hill's shop originally opened at 27 Spencer Road and by 1905 occupied both no. 27 and no. 29. Hill's also owned a store on the Strand Road. Merchant tailors, general drapers and outfitters, Hill's stocked a large and fashionable range of ladies and gents ready-made clothing, as well as blankets, flannels and curtain material. Tailoring was carried out on the premises under Mr Hill's personal supervision, with 'style and fit guaranteed'. The boot and shoe department was added when the premises were extended. (*Mrs Nan Hill*)

Noble & Mason's barber's shop, Carlisle Road, 1930s. The gentleman in the middle of the group is Mr Noble. The Nobles also owned a high-class confectionery shop in Foyle Street. (*Mrs Doreen Rice-Wray*)

Edmiston & Co. Ltd, Shipquay Street, 1939. Edmiston & Co. was one of the leading hardware merchants in the city. Wallace Edmiston, the firm's founder, is in the centre of this group wearing a hat, while his son Macrea is on the extreme right. This photograph was taken just before the staff outing to Shrove, County Donegal. (*Bigger and McDonald Collection*)

Patrick McCallion's grocery shop, 228–230 Bishop Street, 1918. Patrick McCallion is standing outside his shop. It was common practice at this time to sell alcohol at a separate counter in the shop, and originally Mr McCallion would have been known as a spirit grocer. (*Mr Charles Logue*)

Frazer, Mitchell & Co., 1940s. These auctioneers were based in Castle Street in premises that were formerly the reading rooms and library. Frazer, Mitchell & Co. specialised in antique furniture and objects d'art. Sales were conducted weekly, usually on a Thursday. (*Bigger and McDonald Collection*)

Advertisements for the Davis Piano and Music Warehouse and Frazer, Mitchell & Co. (*Christian Brothers Souvenir, 1935*)

Staff of the old jail, Bishop Street, 1930s. (*Derry City Council, Heritage and Museum Service*)

The Royal Irish Constabulary at Victoria Barracks, *c.* 1900. These men were responsible for ensuring law and order in the city and are seen here on a dress parade. Mounted troops are to the rear, the county inspector is standing to the left and the sergeant is mid-row at the front. (*Derry City Council, Heritage and Museum Service*)

A worker at Birmingham Sound Reproducers (BSR). This company was the focal point for male workers in the Derry area from 1952 until its closure in 1967, an event that had devastating effects on an already work-starved area. (*Mr Dan O'Donnell*)

Sammy Campbell and colleague at the BSR plant in Bligh's Lane. The company employed 1,200 people and produced parts for record players and tape recorders. The factory was noted for the strong sense of community among the workforce. There were good times and bad – there were seasonal pay-offs when the market was sluggish and good bonuses when productivity peaked. (*Mr Dan O'Donnell*)

George McDaid, Monsey Morrow and Joe Miller, employees of BSR. Monsey Morrow, who lived in Chamberlain Street, was in charge of the stores in the BSR. Renowned for his sharp wit, Monsey was one of the many great characters who worked there. In the background can be seen hand presses in the machine shop. (*Mr Dan O'Donnell*)

The frontage of the fruit and vegetable shop, with a significant display of fresh produce, and the Richmond Bar in Linenhall Street, 1917. The gentleman in the white apron is Mr Edward Gill who is passing on greetings to his brother Martin in Clydeside, Scotland. (*Mr John McCready*)

Friel's Shop in Abbey Street, off William Street, 1950s. This was a typical corner shop that sold a wide variety of necessities and was invaluable to the local residents, many of whom were allowed credit in the shop. This arrangement prevented many families from going hungry. The arrival of the supermarkets saw a decline in the use of such shops. People took their custom to the new stores where cheaper prices and a wider choice of goods proved irresistible. (*University of Ulster Library*)

A dog receiving a treat from a street vendor in William Street outside the premises of James McGeady's grocery shop, 1920s. This cart states that he is selling 'Pure ice cream'. (*Mrs Margaret Brown*)

Overleaf: This group of schoolgirls is gathered to make a presentation to Miss Magill on her retirement from the Chapel Road Primary School in 1970. (*Miss Magill*)

The Seagate factory at Springtown, 2002. With more than 930 employees the Californian-based Seagate Technologies is one of Derry's largest employers. The company manufactures computer hardware and also hosts a key research and development unit. The opening of the Seagate factory in Londonderry in 1994 was a major economic boost at a crucial time of regeneration for the city. (*Department of the Environment*)

The Dupont site situated at Maydown on the outskirts of the city, early 1990s. Built originally to manufacture Neoprene, a synthetic rubber, production began in 1960. The company now makes two products, Kevlar® and Lycra® and is still a major employer in the area. (*DuPont (UK) Ltd*)

The Foyle Bridge under construction, 1983. The bridge is nearing completion with just the central span to be installed. It opened in 1984 in order to facilitate the flow of traffic through and around the city. (*WELB*)

Workers at the Foyle Bridge, 1984. When completed the bridge was officially named and opened by the then Secretary of State Mr Douglas Hurd at a simple ceremony. It has won the praise of engineering experts as an outstanding achievement, and has also earned the commendation of many artistic organisations for its aesthetic qualities. Grahams in association with Freeman, Fox and Partners built the structure. The engineers were Ove Arup and Partners. (*WELB*)

Grave diggers at the City Cemetery, *c.* 1990. This cemetery must surely be one of the most beautifully situated in Ireland. Laid out on the slope of a hill on the western side of the city, the view of the city and Donegal beyond is amazing and quite breathtaking. As one Derry wit said, 'It's worth being buried up here for the view alone!' (*Mr Eamon Melaugh*)

4

Entertainment

Generations of Derry performers, 15 December 1970. Derry has long been regarded as a city that has nurtured and produced much musical talent and some of this is seen here. Front row, left to right: Joseph Locke, Majella Brady, Dana, Phil Coulter; middle row: Michael O'Duffy, Wee Willie Doherty, James McCafferty; back row: Johnny McCauley, Peter Roddy of the Trend Showband, Patrick O'Hagan. (*Mr Pat McCafferty*)

Little Gaelic Singers, 1956. The group was formed in 1956 and during the next seven years they toured the USA four times and England twice. They were generally acknowledged to be the finest junior choral ensemble ever to originate in Derry and exemplified the creative genius of James McCafferty, their musical director, Tommy Carr, their producer, and Brendan De Glin, their choreographer. While in the USA the young singers, aged between seven and twelve, sang with well-known celebrities such as Elvis Presley and Bing Crosby. (*Mr Pat McCafferty*)

St Eugene's mixed choir, 1948. The members of local choirs paid a small weekly sum for membership. There was keen rivalry between the choirs and even keener competition at the local feis, the annual musical festival, and other competitions. St Eugene's conductor Mr James McCafferty was one of the most celebrated and respected musicians in the city. He had unparalleled success in his career with not only the Little Gaelic Singers but also a number of choirs. He displayed his creative genius in his production of a significant number of concerts and pantomimes. (*Mr Pat McCafferty*)

The choir made up of employees from the Hill's shops in Derry, 1940s. Choral singing has always been a popular pastime in the city. (*Mrs Nan Hill*)

Performers on stage at the opera house, Carlisle Road, *c*. 1920. In its heyday the opera house attracted major performances. Similar in design to the Gaiety Theatre in Dublin, great comfort awaited those who could afford the luxury of seats in the upper circle and the stalls. But it was seats in the gallery, which were known as the Gods, for the majority of the patrons. In the hard times of the 1920s as audience numbers fell and expenses grew the opera house became a cinema. Refurbished in the 1930s, it was gutted by fire in 1940. (*Mr Pat McCafferty*)

A performance of *Trial by Jury* by the Londonderry Operatic Society, 1963. The group continues to stage annual productions that delight the Derry audiences. (*Mrs Nan Hill*)

A dramatic production by Foyle College, 1920. Amateur dramatics has always enjoyed an enthusiastic following in the city. Often this was nurtured in the local schools where drama groups were formed and soon these groups were putting on shows. To this day many local schools stage annual performances which often attract capacity audiences. (*WELB*)

The cast of a pantomime, St Columb's Hall, 1940. In the 1940s pantomimes became another popular form of entertainment in the city and remain so to the present day. The scripts were usually written locally and were full of topical and local allusions that greatly amused the often capacity audiences. Included in this photograph are Leo O'Donnell, Cissie Parlour, Eddie O'Doherty, Neil Murray, Brendan De Glin, Bridie McGuinness, Jimmy Duffy, John Cowley and Dorette Gillen. (*Mrs Dorette Gillen*)

The children's chorus line in one of the local pantomimes, which provided colour, music and dance. Included in this photograph taken in 1948 are Marianna McCafferty, Anne McGeady, Philomena Hegarty, Una McCafferty, Dorothy Brown, Maire McGrory, Ann McCabe, Betty McGeady, Maire Bonar, Sheila Lynch, Helen Gallagher, Gabrielle Doherty, Rosemary McCabe, Anne Devlin, Albina Duddy, Sadie Kitson, Eileen McGeehan and Mary Gillespie. (*Mrs Gabrielle Deans*)

City of Derry Drama Festival presentations, 1970s. On the left is Mr Michael Gillen. Amateur dramatics has always enjoyed a dedicated following in the city. In the latter part of the 1930s drama festivals began and these were instrumental in stimulating and maintaining interest in this form of entertainment. (*Mrs Dorette Gillen*)

Irish dancers, *c.* 1920. The Irish and cultural renaissance of the early 1900s sparked off interest in Gaelic sports, music and dancing. Irish dancing was particularly popular in the city and from the mid-1930s there was a host of Irish dancing schools. Teachers of the calibre of Nellie Sweeney, Brendan De Glin, Lillian O'More, Eugene O'Donnell and Mary McLaughlin soon enjoyed great respect far beyond the confines of the city. Left to right: Mary McDaid, Mary Walker (née Friel) and Maggie Daly. (*Mr Mickey Gillespie*)

Celine O'Donnell (née Quigley), on the left, and Dorette Gillen (née Given) at the Ulster Championships, 1947. This and the photograph opposite illustrate how Irish dancing costumes changed considerably in almost three decades. (*Mrs Dorette Gillen*)

Champion dancers, 1950s. From left: George Kilkie, Noeleen Breslin (née McGovern), Frank Roddy, Grace Doherty (née McGuinness), Raymond O'Connor, Anna Herron, Bernard Boyle and Marie Barrett. (*Mrs Lillian O'More*)

Farewell dance of the 9th Derry Heavy Artillery Regiment, October 1939. During the Second World War dances like these were common prior to the soldiers departing for action. This particular regiment fought in North Africa. (*Bigger and McDonald Collection*)

Dancing in the Corinthian Ballroom, Bishop Street, 1950s. For many young people of the city the regular weekly or nightly dances, or ceilithe were their main source of entertainment. These events were held in halls all over the city. The Corinthian Ballroom was one of the most popular in town and played host to many of the showbands including the Melville Band. (*Mrs Tricia Ward*)

British Legion dance in the Guildhall, 1940s. (*Londonderry Sentinel*)

The Britannia Band, 1925. This ensemble was formed in 1866 as a flute band but changed to brass in 1875 and finally added some reeds years later. It participated fully in the civic and social events in the city during the twentieth century. (*Bigger and McDonald Collection*)

St Columb's Brass and Reed Band, 1929. This band was formed in 1874 under the direction of Mr P. Mulholland who was then organist in St Eugene's Cathedral. It was initially formed by St Columb's Temperance Association to steer people's energy and free time away from alcohol abuse to more constructive pastimes. Fine musicians have come from the ranks of the band, the MacIntyre Brothers, Johnny Quigley and Jackie Bonner. In the centre of the front row are the Revd Neil Farren (furthest right of the two seated clergymen), former president of St Columb's College and later Bishop of Derry, and William 'Pope' Gallagher (seated third from right). (*Mr Charles Logue*)

Hamilton Flute Band, 1930s. The Hamilton Band was formed in 1856 and was known as the 'Primrose Flute' and then the 'Queen Victoria Flute Band'. The name was eventually changed to its present title in honour of the Duke of Abercorn, James Hamilton, Marquis of Londonderry, when he became MP for the city. It is believed that during the First World War all the members of the band joined the 10th Inniskilling Fusiliers and became the regimental band of the 'Derrys'. Today the band is regarded as one of the finest in Northern Ireland. (*Bigger and McDonald Collection*)

Richmond Flute Band, 1930s. This band was based in the Richmond Hall beside Claremont church. Included are J. Shannon (seated third from right), Norman Burnside (seated first on left) and R.J. Finlay (seated second from left). (*Bigger and McDonald Collection*)

Melville Band giving a performance at the Melville Hotel, 1935. The Melville Band was one of the most popular in the city in the 1930s. Those seen here are Jimmy, Willie and Josie McIntyre, Jack Ayling and Freddie Robinson. (*Bigger and McDonald Collection*)

The Carlton Swingtette dance band playing in the Corinthian Ballroom. In 1948 the band took up residence in the Corinthian Ballroom and attracted a large and enthusiastic audience. With their talented vocalist Mick McWilliams and their rhythmic renditions of such numbers as *Black Magic* and *You Go To My Head*, the Carlton Swingtettes entertained the dance-going Derry public until the mid-1950s. (*Mr Pat McCafferty*)

Gay McIntyre and band. This group played the Irish circuit for many years and established a reputation as one of the finest jazz bands ever to come out of Ireland. Former members of the band are Gerry Anderson, BBC presenter, and Colm Arbuckle, Radio Foyle producer and presenter. Gay McIntyre himself was regarded as a highly talented artist and was regularly offered chances to join the big bands in the United Kingdom and the USA. He declined all offers – he wanted to stay in Derry. From left: J. McCallum, Gay McIntyre, Jack Molloy, Sean Canning (*Mr Sean Canning*)

William Loughlin. An outstanding
bass baritone, Mr Loughlin's
contribution to the local music
scene was recognised in 2001
when he was deservedly awarded
the MBE. (*Mr William Loughlin*)

A local Fleadh Cheoil. A festival of
traditional music, song and dance held in
towns and villages throughout Ireland
organised by Comhaltas Ceoltoiri Eireann.
Traditional musicians come to the fleadh
to play, exchange tunes and participate in
competitions. Included in the photograph
is Mr Fintan Vallely, flute player, a
distinguished Irish musician. (*Mr Eamon
Melaugh*)

The Undertones, undoubtedly one of the most successful bands to come out of Derry and indeed Ireland. Between 1978 and 1981 they had a string of hits, with classics such as *Teenage Kicks*, *Jimmy Jimmy* and *My Perfect Cousin*. The band enjoyed a considerable following in Ireland, the United Kingdom and beyond and gained critical acclaim wherever they went. They played their last concert in the summer of 1983 at Punchestown Racecourse but have since played a number of reunion gigs in the city. Left to right: Billy Doherty, Michael Bradley, Feargal Sharkey, Damien O'Neill and John O'Neill (*Mr Michael Bradley*)

Halloween celebrations, 2001. Halloween has become a major event in the city and revellers come from all over the country to take part in this major festival of light. (*Derry City Council*)

5
Politics

First anniversary Bloody Sunday commemoration march, January 1973. On 30 January 1972 thirteen people died when the British Army opened fire on civil rights marchers in Derry's Bogside. The event has been commemorated annually ever since. This photograph shows relatives displaying posters of the victims. (*Mr Eamon Melaugh*)

Explosion at Waterloo
Place, 1973. For almost
three decades scenes of
devastation like this one
were part of life in the city.
All these properties are
still standing today and
the businesses are trading
in what is now a
pedestrian zone. (*DOE*)

King Billy, the William of Orange mural on the Fountain Estate. The murals seen on this postcard were painted by Bobbie Jackson senior in the 1940s and depict King William III crossing the Boyne and the Relief of Derry. The custom of pictorially representing King Billy on gable-end walls is peculiar to Northern Ireland and many of these vivid images have been reproduced as postcards. Fountain Street was renowned as having the best King Billy murals in the province. (*Glen Photography, Dundalk*)

Taken in 1988, this photograph of Kennedy Place on the Fountain Estate demonstrates the concern of the small Protestant community who lived in the city throughout the Troubles. David Jackson painted this Loyalist message and it is clear that the events of the Great Siege are still used as inspiration. The rallying call of Colonel Adam Murray and the citizens of Londonderry was 'No Surrender' and this traditional expression of defiance is still widely used in Loyalist murals. (*Mr Charles Logue*)

"The Apprentice Boys
and No Surrender."
Walker Inciting
The Apprentice Boys to shut the gates of Derry.

A postcard depicting one of the most important historical events in the history of the city of Londonderry. The Apprentice Boys closed the gates on 12 August 1689 thus starting the famous Great Siege and this is commemorated every year by a march and a church service in St Columb's Cathedral. (*WELB*)

"THE PROTESTANT BOYS
WILL CARRY THE DRUMS."

A postcard celebrating the annual Twelfth of July
marches. It is interesting to note the mixture of flat
hats and bowlers in this historic card. Bowlers are now
the accepted headgear for the occasion. (*WELB*)

Tommy Kelly, well known as a street painter, led a
group of Catholic and Protestant children in a joint
project to paint murals. These works of art reflected the
political affiliations of the disparate communities in the
largely Nationalist Shantallow and the Loyalist
Fountain area. (*Mr Eamon Melaugh*)

Free Derry Corner, 1970s. This gable wall became a focal point for the outdoor meetings and rallies that were a regular feature in the Bogside. Free Derry was an area of the Bogside that the RUC and the British Army did not enter for the three-year period between 1969 and 1972. This area has been redeveloped and only the wall remains as a symbol of the struggle for civil rights. (*Mr F. McMenamin*)

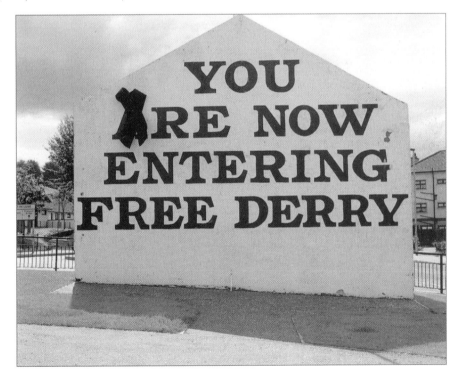

The Free Derry wall as it is today after redevelopment in the area has left it standing as a famous landmark in the Bogside. It has been used to portray many political messages but it is this one that remains the most famous image of the Republican struggle in Derry. (*Cathal Joseph*)

The Derry Citizens' Action Committee march, 16 November 1968. The committee was formed in October 1968 to pressurise the Stormont government to address long-standing local grievances and an unfair electoral system. The march was in direct defiance of a ban by the Unionist government and led some 15,000 people across Craigavon

Bridge to the city centre. Included are Roddy Carlin, Johnny White, Fionnbarra O'Dochartaigh, Michael Canavan, Billy Kelso, Ivan Cooper, John Hume, James Doherty, Brian Patten, Claude Wilton, Brendan Hinds, Aidan McKinney and Vinnie Coyle. (*Ulster Museum Archive*)

The funeral of IRA volunteer Gerard Logue in the Bogside, 24 March 1987. Police Landrovers block the fly-over as soldiers patrol the Lecky Road. Security was tight as the service was taking place in the Long Tower church. On the back of the card is printed 'Despite 22 years of occupation and daily harassment, the will of the Irish people to achieve self-determination remains unbroken.' (*Free Derry Publications*)

This postcard was used to highlight the dispute between local residents and the British Army in the Rosemount area of the city in the early 1990s. The residents felt that their privacy was being invaded by the presence of this watch-tower. On the reverse of the card is printed 'We can't open the curtains any more because we know they're there watching . . . watching 24 hours a day, every day.' Rosemount resident. (*Pat Finucane Centre*)

A section from the banner designed by David Jacques to mark the twentieth anniversary of Bloody Sunday. The idea for it was derived from a photograph taken by Clive Limpkin during rioting in 1969 and has come to symbolise the Battle of the Bogside. Behind the boy can be seen the Rossville flats, the first high flats to be built outside Belfast and now demolished. (*Free Derry Publications*)

Locky Morris' *Statelet*. This depicts a working-class community being imprisoned by the beams of light from the military helicopters overhead. The artist was born in Derry in 1960, one of a generation who grew up during troubled times. His work reflects the changing political situation in the city in which he still lives and works. Recently he designed an innovative public art project entitled 'Points of Departure', which marks six significant periods in the history of the River Foyle. Locky Morris is also a talented musician. (*Free Derry Publications*)

A gently humorous card taking a satirical look at the political divide. The photograph is taken from Waterside railway station looking across the River Foyle to Cityside. Gerry Anderson, a local broadcaster, coined the phrase 'Stroke City'. (*Alan Johnston*)

Londonderry's coat of arms. The skeleton represents Walter de Burgo, a young Anglo-Norman knight. He had a quarrel with his cousin who imprisoned him in the dungeon of the family castle at Greencastle, County Donegal, where he starved to death in 1332. Walter's uncle, Richard de Burgo, had been granted perpetual ownership of Inishowen and the Island of Derry in 1311. The sword of St Paul and the cross of St George are the original arms of the City of London and were added at the time of the Plantation. '*Vita Veritas Victoria*' means 'Life, Truth and Victory'. (*WELB*)

ACKNOWLEDGEMENTS

We wish to express our most sincere thanks to the following people for their help in the compilation of this book and for access to their collections of photographs.

Ian Bartlett, David Bigger, Michael Bradley, Margaret Brown, John Bryson, Sean Canning, Mrs Carlin, Leo Coyle, Gerry Craig, Tony Crowe, Phil Cunningham, Gabrielle Deans, Cathal Doherty, Ken Gamble, Judy Gilfillan, Dorette Gillen, Michael Gillespie, Pearse Henderson, Nan Hill, Paul Kavanagh, William Loughlin, Gerry Lynch, Patricia McAdams, Pat McCafferty, Roy McCullagh, Thelma McDonnell, John McCready, Michael McGuinness, Gay McIntyre, Joe McLaughlin, Frankie McMenamin, T. McQuilkin, Miss Magill, Annesley Malley, Eamon Melaugh, Don Morrison, Joe Nicholas, Dan O'Donnell, Lillian O'More, Billy Platt, Gerry Quinn, Doreen Rice-Wray, Mrs Stanley, Marie Elaine Tierney, Bobby Upton, Charlotte Vij, Bernadette Walsh and Tricia Ward.

We are grateful to the Linenhall Library, the Pat Finucane Centre, Derry City Council Heritage and Museum Services, Magee University, *Londonderry Sentinel*, Department of the Environment, the Heritage Lottery Fund, Ulster Folk and Transport Museum, Bigger and McDonald Collection. A special word of thanks to the staff of the Central Library in Derry for their help and support.

We have tried to ensure all photographs have been correctly credited. We would like to apologise in advance if errors have been made and will make note of any necessary changes.

BIBLIOGRAPHY

Bigger, David and McDonald, Terence. *In Sunshine or in Shadows*, Belfast, Friar's Bush Press, 1990
Bryson, John G. *The Streets of Derry (1625–2001)*, Derry, Guildhall Press, 2001
Cavanagh, Colm. *Derry Jail*, Derry, Guildhall Press, 1982
Christian Brothers Souvenir and Prospectus, Derry, Christian Brothers, 1927
Clements, Roy. *Memory of Memories of Derry*, Derry, Guildhall Press, 1994
Gallagher, Charles. *Acorns and Oakleaf – A Derry Childhood*, Derry, Dubh Regles Books, 1981
Goodman, Jim and Bartlett, Ian. *Britania Band, Londonderry 1866– 1985*, Derry, Britania Band, 1985
Gordon, C.W. *Reminiscences of Derry in the Last Century*, Derry, C.W. Gordon, 1946
Hamilton, Roy. *100 Years of Derry*, Belfast, Blackstaff Press, 1999
Hughes, Sam. *City on the Foyle*, Derry, Ogmios Press, 1984
Lacey, Brian, *Siege City: the Story of Derry and Londonderry*, Belfast, Blackstaff Press, 1990
——. *Discover Derry*, Dublin, O'Brien Press, 1999
McCarter, Geraldine. *Derry's Shirt Tail*, Derry, Guildhall Press, 1991
McCourt, Harry. *Oh How We Danced*, Derry, Guildhall Press, 1992
McFadden, Vera, *Island City*, Leberg Press, 1982
McGuinness, M. and Downey, G. *Creggan*, Derry, Guildhall Press, 2000
Mitchell, Brian. *On the Banks of the Foyle*, Belfast, Friar's Bush Press, 1989
——. *Derry A City Invincible*, Eglinton, Grocers' Hall Press, 1990
Rowan, Alistair. *North-West: the Counties of Londonderry, Donegal, Fermanagh and Tyrone*, Harmonsworth, Penguin, 1979